Let's Catch a Fish!

by Jack Stokes

HENRY Z. WALCK, INC. • NEW YORK

Copyright © 1974 by Jack Stokes. All rights reserved. ISBN: 0-8098-1216-9. LC: 73-19908.
Printed in the United States of America. Cataloging in Publication Data can be found on p. 32.

How
would you like
to catch a big fish?

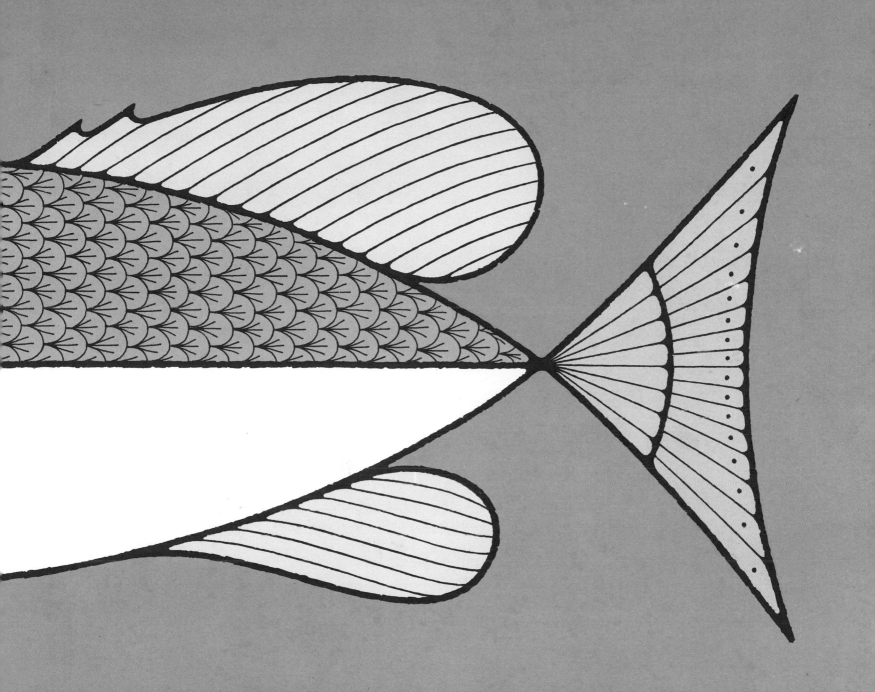

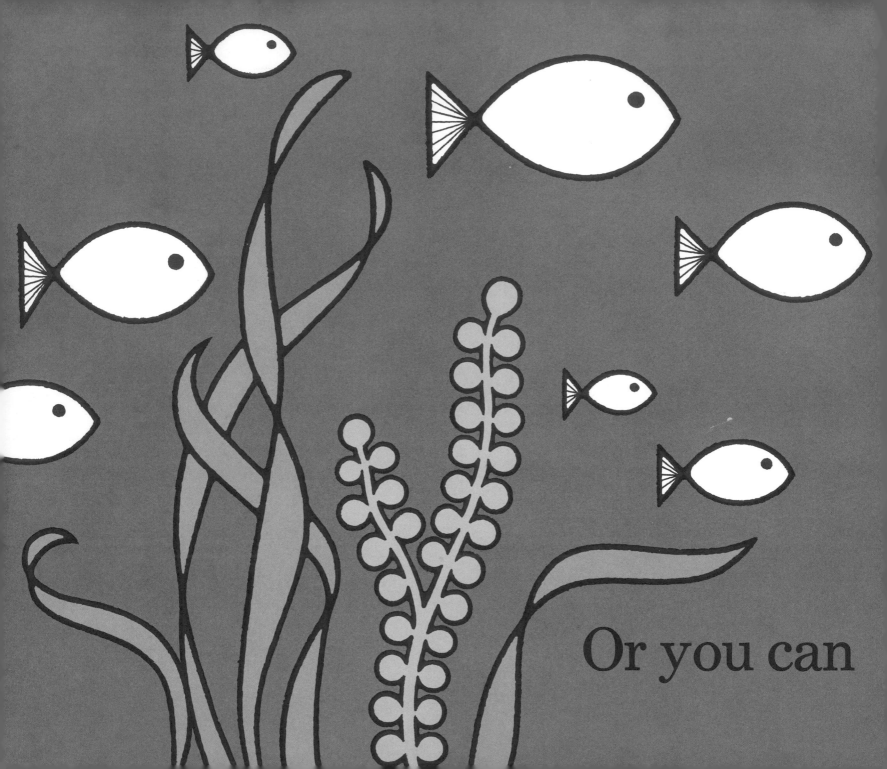

Or you can

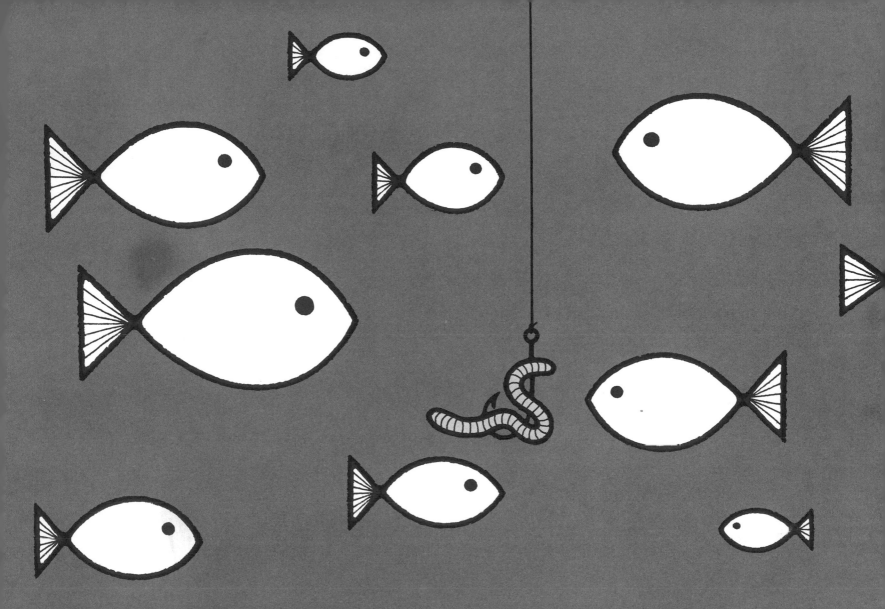

catch smaller ones if you wish.

They come in all colors
and all shapes and sizes;
Fishing is fun
and so full of surprises.

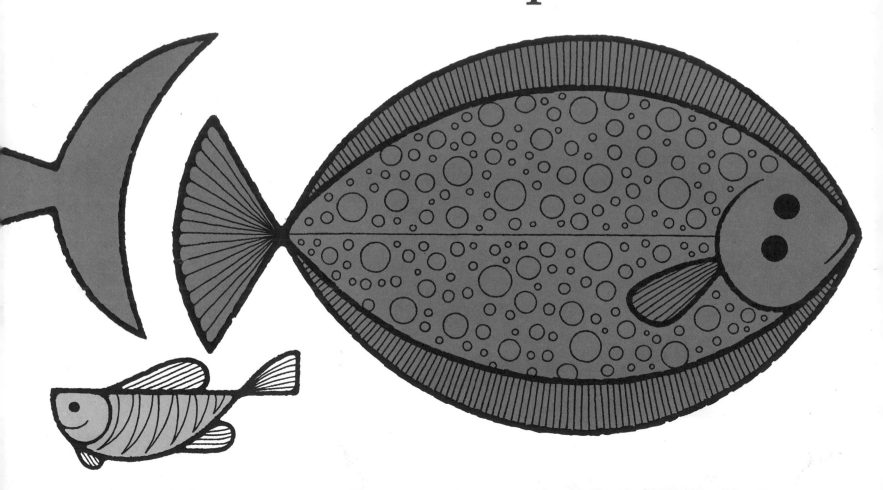

There's a lot to do now, so let us begin.

You can buy a fishhook
or bend a small pin.

Take your line, or a long

piece of string will do too.

Tie it on very tight so the hook

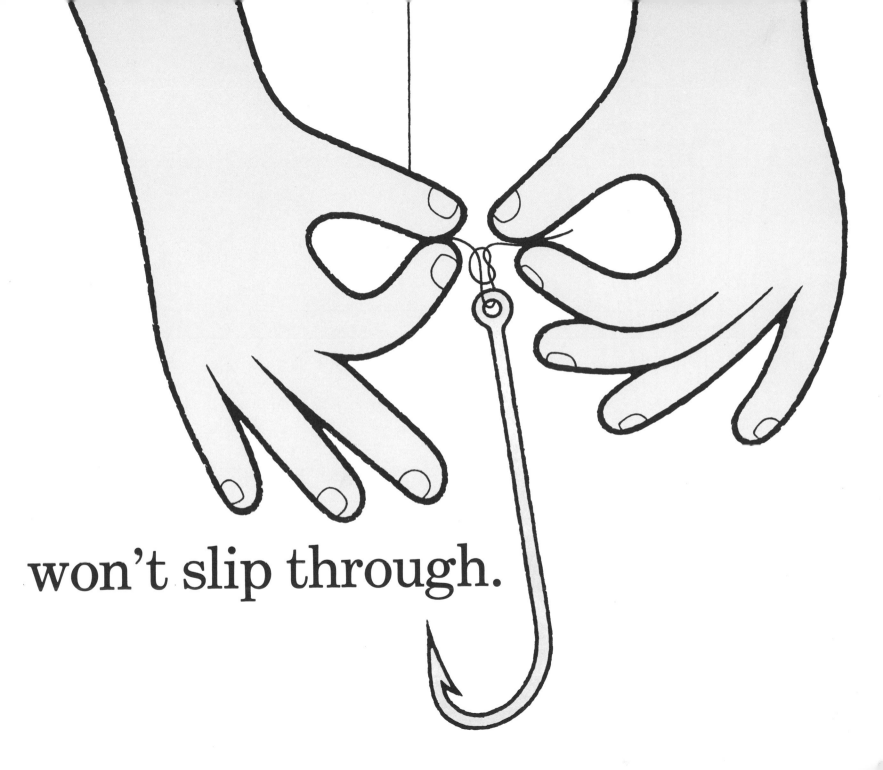

won't slip through.

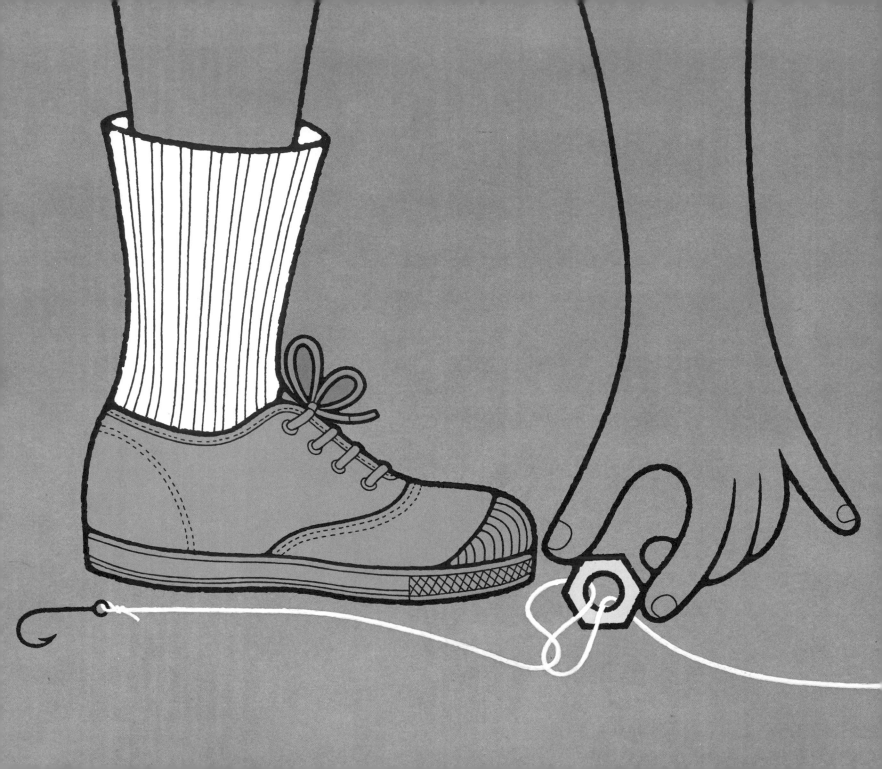

Next fasten the sinker—
or a small metal thing—
A foot from the hook
so it pulls down the string.

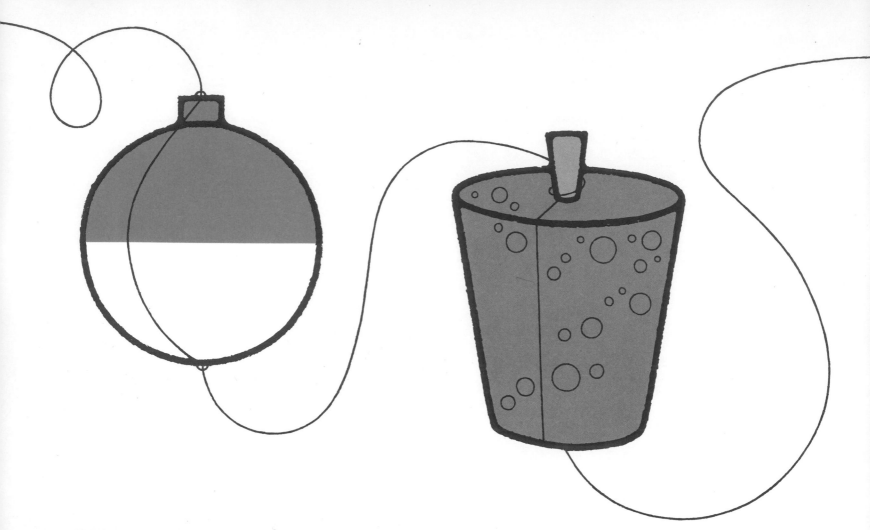

Buy a bobber, or find an old cork

Slip this float on the line, about

the same size.
up to your eyes.

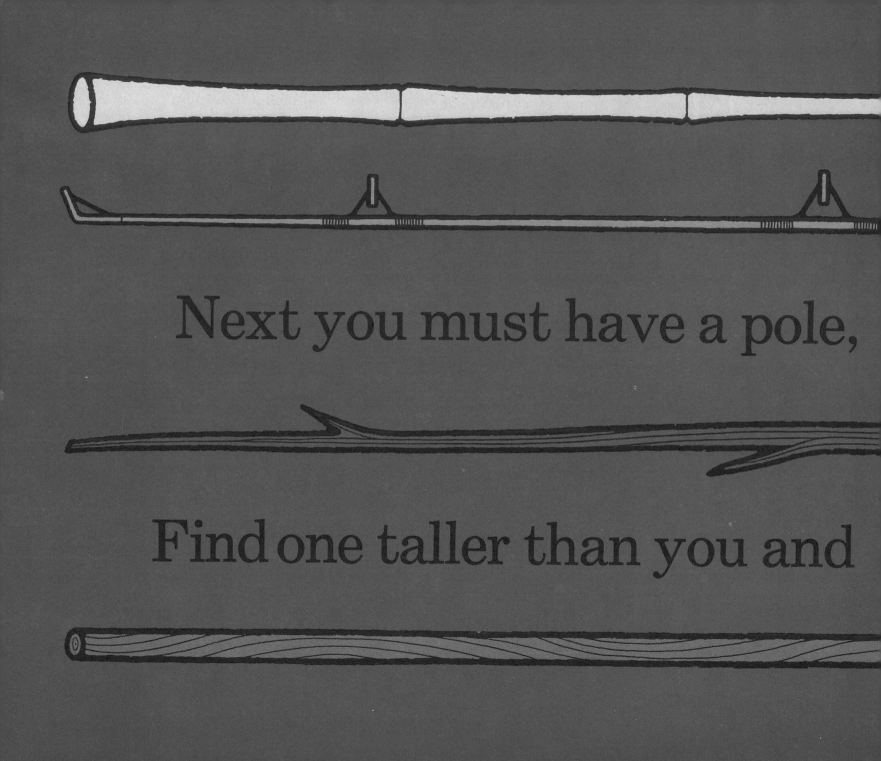

Next you must have a pole,

Find one taller than you and

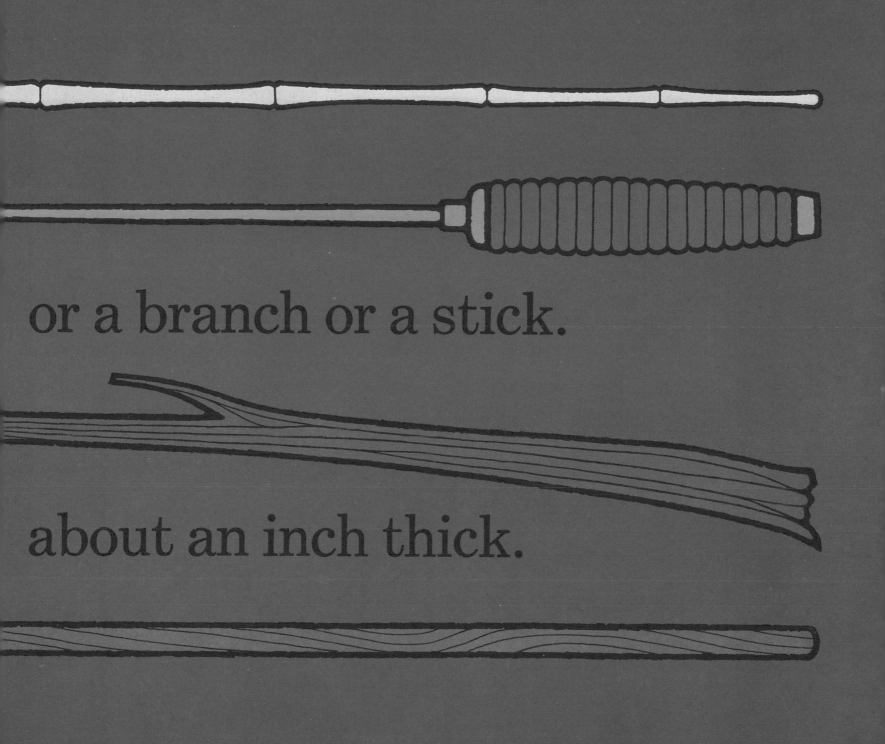

or a branch or a stick.

about an inch thick.

Mark your line from the bobber,
and tie it on tight.
As high as a grown-up
should be about right.

Use a bug or a worm
on the hook for your bait.
For bringing your catch home
a pail is just great.

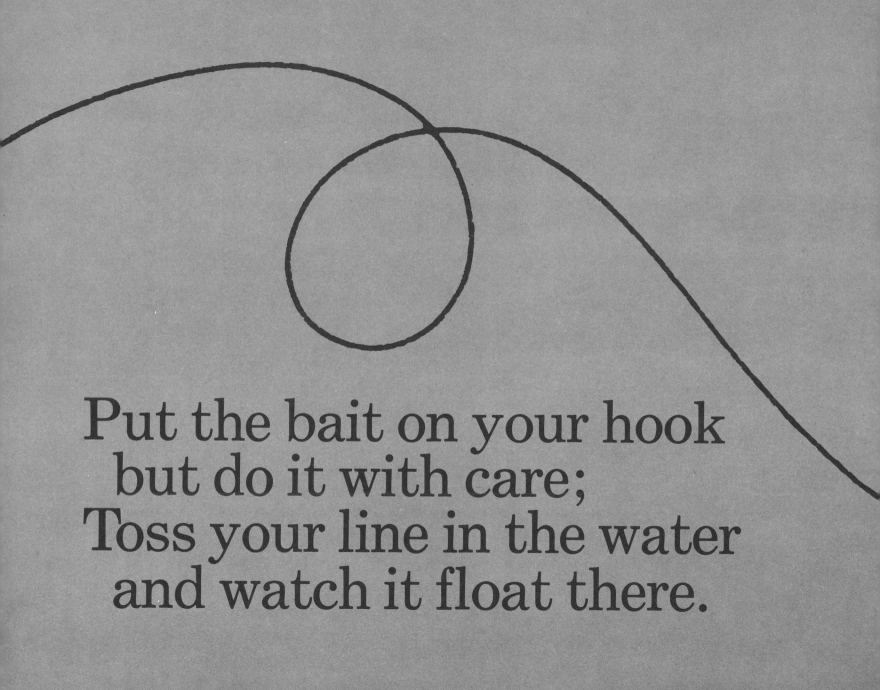

Put the bait on your hook
but do it with care;
Toss your line in the water
and watch it float there.

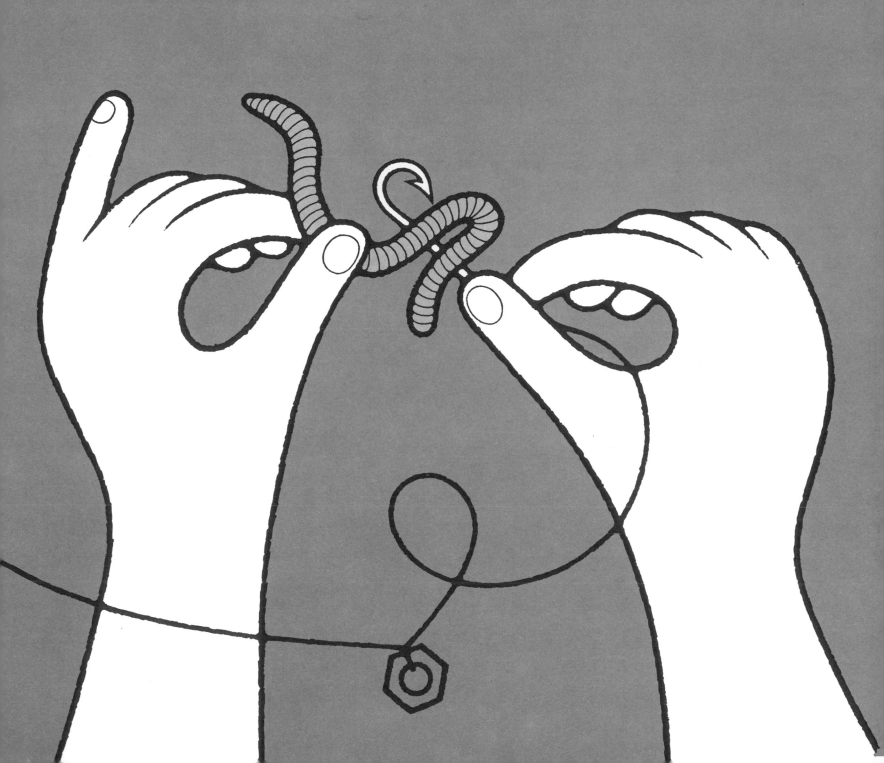

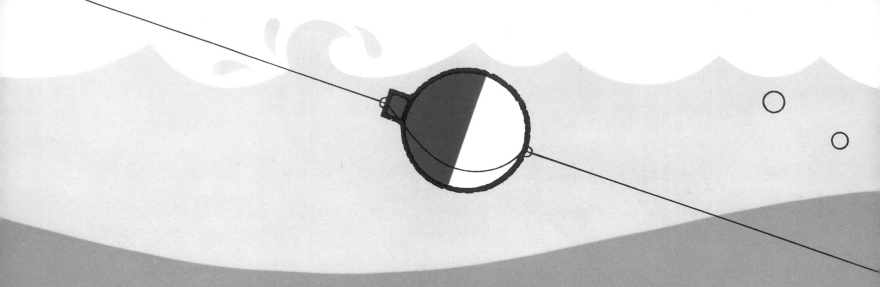

Then with luck there will be
a sharp tug on your line.
Let the bobber go under;
you'll hook him just fine.

Now pull in the line
A wiggling and

and you've gotten your wish—
flopping and slippery fish.

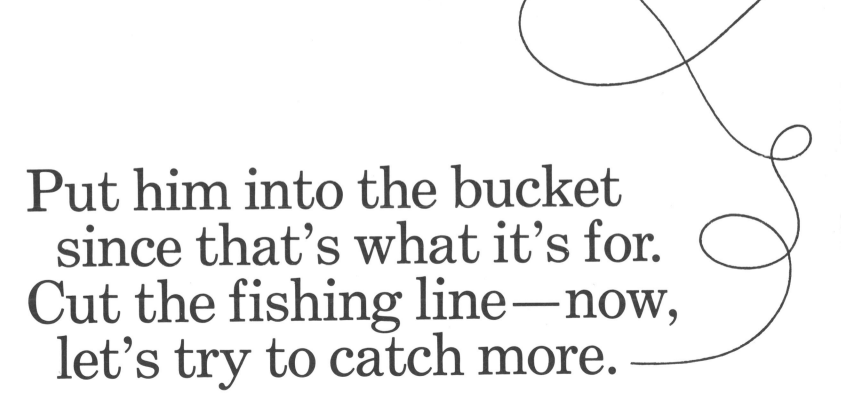

Put him into the bucket
since that's what it's for.
Cut the fishing line—now,
let's try to catch more.

Library of Congress Cataloging in Publication Data

Stokes, Jack.
    Let's catch a fish!

    SUMMARY: Introduces in verse the basics
of fishing from attaching the sinker to pulling
in the fish.
    1. Fishing—Juvenile literature. [1. Fish-
ing] I. Title.
SH445.S86   799.1   73-19908
ISBN 0-8098-1216-9